Pebble™

My World

In My
Town

by Mari C. Schuh

Consulting Editor: Gail Saunders-Smith, PhD
Consultant: Susan B. Neuman, EdD
Former U.S. Assistant Secretary for Elementary
and Secondary Education
Professor, Educational Studies, University of Michigan

Capstone
press

Mankato, Minnesota

Pebble Books are published by Capstone Press,
151 Good Counsel Drive, P.O. Box 669, Mankato, Minnesota 56002.
www.capstonepress.com

1 2 3 4 5 6 10 09 08 07 06 05

Library of Congress Cataloging-in-Publication Data
Schuh, Mari C., 1975–
    In my town / by Mari C. Schuh.
    p. cm.—(Pebble Books. My world)
    Includes bibliographical references and index.
    ISBN 0-7368-4241-1 (hardcover)
    1. Cities and towns—Juvenile literature. 2. City and town life—Juvenile
literature. I. Title. II. Series: My world (Mankato, Minn.)
HT152.S38 2006
307.76—dc22   2004030040

Summary: Simple text and photographs introduce basic community concepts related
to towns including location, things in a town, and different types of towns.

Note to Parents and Teachers

The My World set supports national social studies standards related
to communities. This book describes and illustrates towns.
The images support early readers in understanding the text.
The repetition of words and phrases helps early readers learn new
words. This book also introduces early readers to subject-specific
vocabulary words, which are defined in the Glossary section. Early
readers may need assistance to read some words and to use the
Table of Contents, Glossary, Read More, Internet Sites, and Index
sections of the book.

Table of Contents

My Town

I live in a town.
My town has
many buildings
and neighborhoods.

My town is in a state
called Iowa.
My state has many towns.

Places in My Town

My town has
a post office.
I mail letters
to my grandma.

My town has a library.
I pick out books and
use the computers.

My town has
a police station.
Police officers help keep
our town safe.

Other Towns

Some towns are small.
Only a few hundred
people live in them.

Big towns
are called cities.
Big cities can have
millions of people living
in them.

Towns are found
around the world.
Towns look different
in other countries.

Every town is different.
What is your town like?

Glossary

library—a place where books and other materials are kept for reading or borrowing; many libraries have computers that people use to find information on the Internet.

neighborhood—a small area in a town or city where people live

police officer—a person who is trained to keep people safe and make sure laws are obeyed

post office—a building where people go to buy stamps and send letters and packages

state—an area of land with borders you can see only on a map; each state can make some of their own laws; the United States has 50 states.

town—a group of neighborhoods that form a community; towns are smaller parts of a state.

Read More

Holland, Gini. *I Live in a Town.* Where I Live. Milwaukee: Weekly Reader Early Learning Library, 2004.

Kehoe, Stasia Ward. *I Live in a City.* Kids in Their Communities. New York: PowerKids Press, 2000.

Nelson, Robin. *Where Is My Town?* First Step Nonfiction. Minneapolis: Lerner, 2002.

Internet Sites

FactHound offers a safe, fun way to find Internet sites related to this book. All of the sites on FactHound have been researched by our staff.

Here's how:

1. Visit *www.facthound.com*
2. Type in this special code **0736842411** for age-appropriate sites. Or enter a search word related to this book for a more general search.
3. Click on the **Fetch It** button.

FactHound will fetch the best sites for you!

Index

Word Count: 111
Grade: 1
Early-Intervention Level: 10

Editorial Credits

Heather Adamson, editor; Juliette Peters, designer and illustrator; Jo Miller,
    photo researcher; Scott Thoms, photo editor

Photo Credits

Bruce Coleman Inc./Andrew Rakoczy, 14
Capstone Press/Karon Dubke, cover, 1, 4, 8, 10, 12, 20
DAVID R. FRAZIER Photolibrary, 16
Index Stock Imagery/Michele Burgess, 18

The author dedicates this book to the Royce family of Mapleton, Minnesota, who have
helped her call Mapleton home.